Hispanic Heritage

Hispanic Heritage

Title List

Puerto Ricans' History and Promise

Americans Who Cannot Vote

by Jim Stafford

Mason Crest Publishers
Philadelphia

Mason Crest Publishers Inc.

370 Reed Road

Broomall, Pennsylvania 19008

(866) MCP-BOOK (toll free)

First printing

1 2 3 4 5 6 7 8 9 10

Library of Congress Cataloging-in-Publication Data

Stafford, Jim, 1963-

  Puerto Ricans' history and promise : Americans who cannot vote / by Jim Stafford.

      p. cm. —— (Hispanic heritage)

  Includes index.

  ISBN 1-59084-927-2   ISBN 1-59084-924-8 (series)

  1. Puerto Ricans—History. 2. Puerto Ricans—Biography. 3. Puerto Rico—History. 4.
Puerto Rico—Relations—United States. 5. United States—Relations—Puerto Rico. I.
Title: Puerto Ricans' history and promise. II. Title. III. Hispanic heritage (Philadelphia,
Pa.)

  F1971.S73 2005

  972.95 — dc22

                    2004021670

Cover design and interior design by Dianne Hodack.

Produced by Harding House Publishing Service, Inc., Vestal, New York.

Printed and bound in the Hashemite Kingdom of Jordan.

Contents

Introduction

by José E. Limón, Ph.D.

ven before there was a United States, Hispanics were present in what would become this country. Beginning in the sixteenth century, Spanish explorers traversed North America, and their explorations encouraged settlement as early as the sixteenth century in what is now northern New Mexico and Florida, and as late as the mid-eighteenth century in what is now southern Texas and California.

Later, in the nineteenth century, following Spain's gradual withdrawal from the New World, Mexico in particular established its own distinctive presence in what is now the southwestern part of the United States, a presence reinforced in the first half of the twentieth century by substantial immigration from that country. At the close of the nineteenth century, the U.S. war with Spain brought Cuba and Puerto Rico into an interactive relationship with the United States, the latter in a special political and economic affiliation with the United States even as American power influenced the course of almost every other Latin American country.

The books in this series remind us of these historical origins, even as each explores the present reality of different Hispanic groups. Some of these books explore the contemporary social origins—what social scientists call the "push" factors—behind the accelerating Hispanic immigration to America: political instability, economic underdevelopment and crisis, environmental degradation, impoverished or wholly absent educational systems, and other circumstances contribute to many Latin Americans deciding they will be better off in the United States.

And, for the most part, they will be. The vast majority come to work and work very hard, in order to earn better wages than they would back home. They fill significant labor needs in the U.S. economy and contribute to the economy through lower consumer prices and sales taxes.

When they leave their home countries, many immigrants may initially fear that they are leaving behind vital and important aspects of their home cultures: the Spanish language, kinship ties, food, music, folklore, and the arts. But as these books also make clear, culture is a fluid thing, and these native cultures are not only brought to America, they are also replenished in the United States in fascinating and novel ways. These books further suggest to us that Hispanic groups enhance American culture as a whole.

Our country—especially the young, future leaders who will read these books—can only benefit by the fair and full knowledge these authors provide about the socio-historical origins and contemporary cultural manifestations of America's Hispanic heritage.

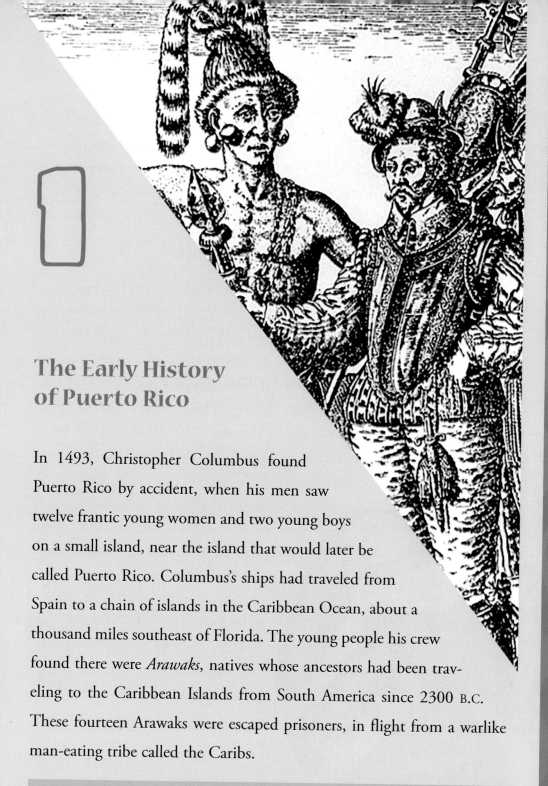

The Early History of Puerto Rico

In 1493, Christopher Columbus found Puerto Rico by accident, when his men saw twelve frantic young women and two young boys on a small island, near the island that would later be called Puerto Rico. Columbus's ships had traveled from Spain to a chain of islands in the Caribbean Ocean, about a thousand miles southeast of Florida. The young people his crew found there were *Arawaks*, natives whose ancestors had been traveling to the Caribbean Islands from South America since 2300 B.C. These fourteen Arawaks were escaped prisoners, in flight from a warlike man-eating tribe called the Caribs.

Artwork

A poster at Hunter College's Centro de Estudios Puertorriqueños celebrates aspects of Puerto Rican culture.

9

commonwealth:
a self-governing
territory.

The distressed Arawaks appeared strange to Columbus and his men. The natives had skin the color of the copper kettles in which Columbus cooked, or like the pennies Americans use today. Members of the group were also much shorter than the Spaniards accompanying Columbus. They had straight black hair, very prominent cheekbones, and they wore jewelry of shells, bones, clay, and gold. Except for the married women, the Arawaks wore no clothes.

Likewise, Columbus's group must have startled these Native people. Columbus and his crew of at least 1,200 men rode in seventeen wooden ships that rose high out of the water. The men wore heavy armor and used weapons such as swords and pistols. The peaceful Arawaks had never imagined such weaponry, nor could they comprehend the Spanish desire for gold.

The Arawaks led Columbus through a series of islands toward a larger island, and as Columbus's ships approached it, the young Natives dove off his ships toward the beaches that led to their homes.

In such a way, Columbus first arrived on the island we know today as *Puerto Rico*. That day began a five-hundred-year struggle for freedom and independence that the island's people continue today. The struggle has involved the Arawaks, who died from war and disease; then later the Africans, who experienced harsh slavery on sugar plantations; the Creoles of mixed race, who farmed in poverty as Spanish subjects for centuries; and finally modern Puerto Ricans, who still struggle for manufacturing jobs and financial security as citizens of an American *commonwealth*.

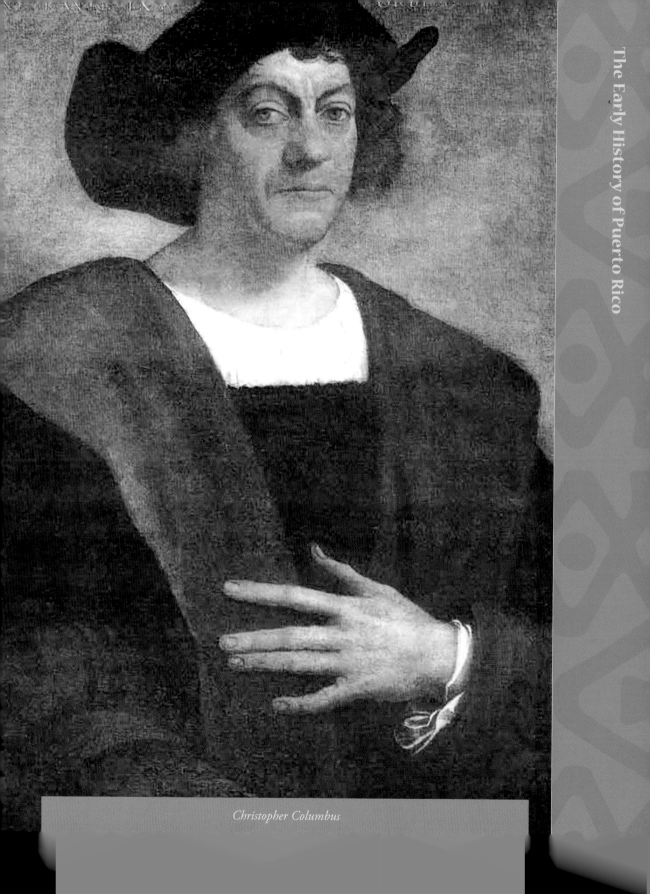

Christopher Columbus

Columbus's ships, the Nina, *the* Pinta, *and the* Santa Maria

A Spanish priest who read Columbus's journal of 1493, describes Columbus's favorable first impression of the cities and people of Boriquen:

Several Christians went ashore and walked to some houses that were very artfully made, although of straw and wood; and there was a plaza, with a road leading to the sea, very clean and straight, made like a street, and the walls were of crossed or woven cane; and above, beautiful gardens, as if they were vineyards or orchards or citron trees, such as there are in Valencia or Barcelona [Spanish cities].

uring this first visit, Columbus entered a village of fifty to a hundred people who slept in *hamaca* (hammocks), drummed on trees, used wooden swords, and dyed their bodies red for important ceremonies. The Arawaks believed in both a supreme God (*Yukaya*) and an evil spirit (*Jurakan*). Today we have inherited the word *hurricane* as a version of the word *Jurakan*. The tribe's leader was called a cacique, a position that was often filled by a woman.

Such villages were scattered throughout the 100-by-35-mile (160.9-by-56.3-kilometer) island, and were connected to one another as a federation, similar to the way the states within the United States make up one larger country today. About 30,000 Arawaks lived on the entire island of Puerto Rico in 1493.

The natives called their island *Boriquen*, which meant *Land of the Noble Lord* in their own language. Columbus called the island *San Juan Bautista*, after Don Juan, the son of Spain's Queen Isabella (who had paid for his expedition), and also after John the Baptist from the Christian Bible.

conquistadors:
Spanish conquerors.

artisans: skilled
craftspeople.

Just as Columbus had re-named Boriquen *San Juan Bautista*, he gave the Arawaks a Spanish name, calling them the *Tainos*.

Columbus's Voyages

This trip in 1493 was Columbus's second voyage to North America. Columbus had first sailed there in three ships in 1492. King Ferdinand and Queen Isabella of Spain had financed that trip because they had hoped he would eventually reach India if he traveled westward over the Atlantic Ocean. The possibility of a quick ocean route to India attracted Spain because for centuries Spaniards had taken long treacherous eastern land routes to China and India—in order to trade for exotic sugar, silks, and spices.

While the men on Columbus's first voyage were explorers—three ships full of sailors and *conquistadors*—the men on Columbus's second voyage were mainly colonizers, men chosen to stay in the Americas and build settlements. These included astronomers, cartographers (mapmakers), *artisans*, and laborers.

Because Columbus wrongly believed that he had traveled around the entire world and found a new part of India, he called the natives he encountered in North America, and on islands such as Puerto Rico, *Indians*. However, the riches Columbus quickly discovered on his second voyage were not the riches of India. They were the plants, fruits, colorful birds, and even gold of Puerto Rico.

Puerto Rico's rich coast

The Spanish Invasion

fter 1493, Columbus left Boriquen forever, and no one from Spain returned for fifteen years. In 1508, a Spaniard named Ponce de Leon (a conquistador who
accompanied Columbus on his first visit) returned to build a fort and to colonize the

The name *Puerto Rico* is a Spanish phrase meaning "rich port." When Columbus first arrived he called only the island's largest city Puerto Rico, and the entire island was *San Juan Bautista*. The Spaniards did not switch the names of the island and its capital city until 1521, long after Columbus's visit. During this later period, the entire island took the name *Puerto Rico*, and the island's capital city became *San Juan Bautista*, or *San Juan*. These names remain today.

island for Spain. Not only did the Spanish claim the island, but they claimed the Arawaks, too. King Ferdinand assigned both land and thirty to three hundred Indians to each of the Spanish colonists. In 1510, the Spanish began to mine gold on the island, forcing the Natives to do the actual work. They also made the Natives wear clothes and study Christianity.

For several years, the Indians worked for the Spanish because they believed the Spanish were immortal. One reason the Indians may have believed this was that the Spaniards did not become sick from diseases as frequently as the Indians did. The Spaniards, because they had brought many of the diseases with them from Europe, had built up a resistance to them.

The ancient fort of San Juan

In the centuries after Columbus landed in the New World in 1492, more native North Americans died each year from infectious diseases brought by the European settlers than were born. Germs were the Indians' worst enemy.

Many types of diseases were brought into the Americas; the main ones were smallpox, measles, influenza, and typhus, as well as whooping cough, mumps, and diphtheria. When a person is exposed to the germs that cause these illnesses, he will usually become ill. If he does not die, however, his body will have created antibodies to protect him from becoming infected again by the same germs. In other words, he will have immunity to that particular germ.

Many types of infectious diseases are carried by animals and passed along to humans. Europeans lived close to various types of domestic animals, and so they had plenty of opportunities to come in contact with many types of infectious disease and develop immunity. Each generation had also developed genetic material that made people more resistant to disease. (Through natural selection, people who have acquired disease-resistant genes are more likely to survive.)

In the Americas, however, there were only a few domesticated animals, which did not carry harmful germs, so the transference of disease from animals to humans was unlikely. In fact, the Americas were considered virtually disease-free. Since North and South America had no exposure to European diseases, severe outbreaks of disease were destined to occur once the newcomers arrived. We will probably never know how many people died as a result of the Europeans' arrival in the Americas.

As the Spanish colonized the Americas, they brought deadly germs with them that spread throughout the Native populations.

smallpox: *a highly contagious disease characterized by high fever and scar-producing sores.*

buccaneers: *pirates who preyed on Spanish colonies and shipping in the West Indies.*

galleons: *large three-masted sailing ships.*

The Indians began to rebel against their Spanish masters in 1510, after a cacique named Uragyoan had his men hold a Spaniard under water for several hours to discover if he could actually be killed. After watching his body for several days for signs of life, the Arawaks revolted on various parts of the island. Ultimately, Ponce de Leon put down the rebellion, ordering six thousand of the Arawaks shot. By 1514, with many of the Arawaks either dead from disease, killed, or escaped to other islands, less than four thousand of the original 30,000 inhabitants of Boriquen remainded.

When Puerto Rico's gold ran out, the Spanish changed the island's economy from mining to agriculture, and began to bring in African slaves to work on sugar plantations. In 1521, when the Spanish King Charles V ordered the freedom of all remaining Indians on the island, only six hundred of them were left.

Several times during the sixteenth century, large groups of Indians and Spaniards died of *smallpox*, brought to the island by African slaves. Also, pirates, as well as the warlike Carib Indians, attacked various settlements on the land, while *buccaneers* from various countries, especially from France, attacked the treasure-filled Spanish *galleons*—loaded with silver, pearls, and all kinds of treasure—that anchored near Puerto Rico before their long trip back to Spain.

The Spaniards' forts still remain.

Spanish Rule

round 1523, sugarcane became the major crop of Puerto Rico, and the Spanish began to build huge forts to protect the island. By 1572, however, Puerto Rico was poor, and existed mainly as a military stronghold, protecting against other countries, like England, who now ruled the oceans. Many Spanish forts, like El Mono and San Cristobel, as well as the eight-foot thick walls around the city, still survive today.

contraband: items
that are illegal.

One of the two largest attacks during this period was by George Clifford (the Earl of Cumberland) of England, who held the entire island for five months in 1598. The other was by the Dutch, who attacked the island in 1625, destroying much of San Juan.

During this period of low economic production, Puerto Rico received an allowance, or *situado*, from Spain. The population of the island was comprised of two very distinct groups of people. There were the Spanish colonists who owned large farms, and there was a growing *Criollo* or Creole culture. The Creole, or Native population, was of mixed race, having descended from Spaniards, Arawaks, and Africans, who had all intermarried. The Creole population grew small cash crops of coffee, cane, and tobacco, and lived in small huts, Indian style. Eventually, their people would be considered a lower class on the island, within a class system that would continue long after slavery was abolished.

During the 1700s and early 1800s, many Creoles developed an illegal *contraband* business with French, British, and Dutch islands. These individuals did not pay taxes to the Spanish government and sold things without the government's consent. The Spanish tried to combat this smuggling, because the government's treasury was empty and the Caribbean was still full of pirates preying on Spanish ships. One way the Spanish tried to regain economic control of their colony was by bringing in coffee, a crop whose growth Spain could oversee, and whose sale they could easily tax.

Pirates were a fact of life in the waters around eighteenth-century Puerto Rico.

Slave ships brought Africans to Puerto Rico.

Harsh Masters

Another way that Spain controlled the people of the island was by ruling them harshly. From 1825 through 1860, the island experienced a period of fourteen very cruel colonial governors sent from Spain. For example, one of the governors, Field Marshall Juan Primm, ordered that any black man who attacked a white man could be executed. If he attacked a free black male he would lose his right hand. If he insulted a white he would receive five years in prison. If two blacks were caught fighting, they got twenty-five lashes and fifteen days in jail. A black who was caught stealing received two lashes and a fine. This law was known as the *Bando Negro*, or Black Edict.

Of the many Puerto Rican uprisings against Spain during this period, the *Grito de Lares* (Cry of the Lares) of 1868 is the most famous. About five hundred rebels, many of them day workers, farmers, and slaves, declared independence from Spain, telling any Spanish settlers living in Puerto Rico that they had three days to declare themselves in favor of the Republic, to leave for Spain, or to accept the punishment reserved for traitors. Although these rebels had gathered five hundred rifles, six canons, and a small ship, they were only able to take over the city of Lares before all of them were jailed, killed, or captured.

A series of compromises followed, in which Spain once again changed its strategy of governing Puerto Rico. In 1869, for the second time, Spain gave the island the right to send representatives to the *Cortes*, the Spanish houses of government. Also, in November 1872, King Asmadeo I de Saloya abolished slavery on the island.

Changes

At this point in Puerto Rico's history there were two main political parties, one that wanted total freedom from Spain and one that wanted to become a part of Spain. When a Spanish terrorist killed Prime Minister Canovas de Castillo in August 1897, Sagasta de Mateo Przxedes rose to power, granting Puerto Rico more freedom, as well as more power within the Spanish government, than it had ever enjoyed. Now the citizens of Puerto Rico could elect *delegates* to both houses of the Spanish Cortes.

Such freedom and power were short lived. Puerto Rico once again changed hands, and its people continued to struggle in new ways against a new ruling nation. Puerto Rico would now be a territory of the United States.

A landmark from Puerto Rico's Spanish history

Habla Español

grito (gree-toe): shout or cry

2

Puerto Rico's Relationship with the United States

In 1898, General Nelson A. Miles landed with 1,600 American soldiers at Guanica. The Spanish American War had begun. The war lasted only seventeen days in Puerto Rico before Spain surrendered. In his first public speech, General Miles said:

> We have not come to make war upon the people of a country that for centuries has been oppressed but on the contrary to bring you protection . . . to promote your prosperity, and to bestow upon you the immunities and blessings of the liberal institutions of our government.

or many years Spain had been a world power. By the late 1800s, however, what had once been a mighty empire had dwindled to a few possessions in the Pacific, Africa, and West Indies. Many of the remaining colonies wanted their independence.

At the same time the Spanish colonies were flexing their muscles to gain independence, a journalistic battle was heating up in the United States. William Randolph Hearst often used the power of his newspaper chain to stir up American opinion in favor of war. He published reports about alleged cruelties committed by the Spanish on the poor "hapless" Cubans. The reports appearing in the Hearst newspapers helped spur Americans to push for war. Added to the need of the U.S. Navy to establish a training base, a lack of activity for the U.S. Army, and the idea of Manifest Destiny, the atmosphere was ripe for war.

As the U.S.S. *Maine* sat in the Havana harbor on February 15, 1898, it exploded, and the battleship sank; a total of 260 men died on the *Maine*. The press was quick to blame Spain for the explosion, and cries of "Remember the Maine!" quickly spread. (It is believed today that the explosion was most likely an accident.) On April 11, 1898,

President William McKinley asked Congress for the authority to send troops to Cuba to end the civil war. On April 25, Congress declared a state of war with Spain.

Future president Theodore Roosevelt was a major military hero of the Spanish-American War. On July 1, 1898, Roosevelt led his company of "Rough Riders" at the Battle of San Juan Hill.

Battles ended on August 12, 1898, when Spain realized that U.S. forces controlled the waterways around Cuba, and the Spanish troops could not be resupplied. The Treaty of Paris formally ended the war on August 12.

Teddy Roosevelt's Rough Riders

The entrance to San Juan harbor

Although the American intervention had ended 405 years of Spain's domination of Puerto Rico, Puerto Rico was now worried that they would become an American colony. They had just won a great amount of home rule from Spain seven years earlier, and they were not looking for a new master.

On December 10, 1898, the Treaty of Paris gave Puerto Rico to the United States. At this time, Puerto Rico had a tiny educated class, a small middle class, and a huge lower class. Only 13 percent of Puerto Rico's citizens could read. Many lived in thatched huts and ate only one small meal a day.

A few months after the United States landed in Puerto Rico, the U.S. Congress passed the Foraker Act, describing America's plan for Puerto Rico:

Puerto Rico will at first be governed by a military regime; then it will be declared an American territory, and later it will achieve the category of sovereign state within the Union. The duration of these periods will depend more or less on the merits of the country.

American Control

he Foraker Act remained in effect from 1900 to 1916. However, the plans described by the act never came to pass. Unlike Alaska and Hawaii, Puerto Rico never became a state of the United States.

Instead, the Foraker Act made the island much like a colony of the United States, the way the original American colonies had belonged to England. The island did not have representation in Congress, and it could not refine any of its raw materials, like sugar, that it provided to the United States.

hen the famous aviator, Charles Lindbergh, landed on their island in 1928, some citizens of Puerto Rico persuaded him to deliver a message to Calvin Coolidge:

Grant us the freedom that you enjoy, for which you struggled, which you worship, which we deserve, and you have promised us.

The citizens of the island continually argued for a *plebiscite* to decide whether Puerto Rico would become a state of the United States, a commonwealth of the United States, or an independent country.

Rebellion

Puerto Rico served as an army base during World War II.

n 1936, the Nationalist Party marched in a Puerto Rican city called Ponce. Their demonstration became violent, leaving a hundred wounded and twenty protesters and two police officers dead. No one knows whether police or demonstrators fired the first shot, but this event is now called the Massacre of Ponce.

Congress ignored Puerto Rico's demands for a plebiscite and instead passed the Jones Act in 1938. This act proclaimed U.S. citizenship for all Puerto Ricans, but many of these new citizens still wanted complete freedom from America; they wanted their island to become an independent nation. The Jones Act also failed to please the Puerto Ricans who wanted the island to become a state of the United States.

In 1940, the Popular Democratic Party led by Luis Munoz Marin gained power. This party was less interested in Puerto Rico's statehood status and much more interested in raising the island's standard of living. The party's slogan was "Bread, Land, and Liberty" and its emblem was the *pava*, the broad straw hat worn by peasants.

In 1948, Puerto Rico developed its own *constitution* under commonwealth status. Two years later, when President Harry S.

Pedro Campos, Puerto Rican political leader

U.S. Army barracks in San Juan, Puerto Rico

Truman declared Puerto Rico a commonwealth, or what is now known as a *free associated state*, many angry members of the Nationalist Party attacked the governor's mansion in old San Juan, peppering it with bullets. Also, two New York–based Puerto Ricans tried to kill President Truman in Washington.

Commonwealth

owever, Puerto Ricans themselves passed Truman's bill in 1951, 387,000 to 119,000, making Puerto Rico a self-governing territory. While Puerto Rican Nationalists defined *freedom* as complete independence from the United States, most Puerto Ricans had begun to define it as the economic security provided by a relationship with the United States.

When President Truman declared Puerto Rico a commonwealth, however, once again Puerto Rican Nationalists attacked violently. In 1954, some of them rose in the U.S. House of Representatives in Washington D.C. Three men and women yelled, *"Viva Puerto Rico libre!"* and sprayed the House floor with bullets, wounding five representatives.

Today's Puerto Rico

oday, although political parties in Puerto Rico still debate its independence, most Puerto Ricans favor the island's commonwealth status. In a 1967 plebiscite, 60 percent of the island's citizens voted for commonwealth status, 39 percent voted for statehood, and only .6 percent favored independence. In a 1993 *referendum*, 46 percent of Puerto Rico's citizens favored statehood, and 48 percent favored commonwealth status.

Today, that commonwealth status allows Puerto Rico to keep more of its independence and culture than statehood would, and at the same time benefit from a close economic relationship with the United States, more than independence would allow. Commonwealth status means that residents of Puerto Rico do not pay federal income tax, or vote for the U.S. President, but that they do pay Social Security, receive federal welfare, and serve in the U.S. armed services.

Since the Arawak people fled the dangerous Carib headhunters, the citizens of Puerto Rico have struggled to be free while living among forces beyond their control. Most people on the island today are themselves descendants of various groups who once fought or enslaved one another. Today, issues of freedom aren't as simple as they were in the past. People no longer discuss slavery, but instead, the issues of social class, economic opportunities, and what the right to govern themselves actually means.

Habla Español

libre (lee-bray): free

independencia (een-day-pane-dane-see-ah): independence

uis Marin's reforms and Puerto Rico's status as a free associated state have both raised Puerto Rico's economic growth above that of other Caribbean communities. In the 1950s, a measure passed by Congress called Operation Bootstrap gave Puerto Rico duty-free access to the United States, as well as tax incentives for businesses to move there. Since the 1950s, U.S. firms have invested heavily in Puerto Rico, and U.S. minimum-wage laws apply there.

Puerto Rico today

3

Current Political, Economic, and Social Conditions in Puerto Rico

In 1999, a disaster on Puerto Rico's tiny island of Vieques drew the entire world's attention. Several American F-18 fighter jets had been practicing combat maneuvers on an uninhabited part of Vieques when they dropped two five-hundred-pound bombs two miles away from their intended targets. Four civilians were injured, and David Sanes Rodriquez, a thirty-five-year-old security guard was killed. The Puerto Rican people were outraged that the U.S. military had accidentally bombed its own citizens.

During the investigation that followed, Puerto Ricans banded together in their protests of the U.S.'s dangerous use of Puerto Rico for combat training. A protest march in the capital of San Juan in February 2000 drew 150,000 people. All three of Puerto Rico's political parties—who usually argued among themselves about whether Puerto Rico should remain a commonwealth, should become America's fifty-first state, or should declare its independence—united to say, "The bomb which killed David Sanes must be the last bomb to fall on Vieques."

From May 1999 until May 2000, Puerto Rican citizens of all political parties took over the island of Vieques, acting as human shields to force an end to the bombing on the island. At the end of the year, the protesters were removed, and fifteen hundred of them were arrested. Katerine McCaffrey writes:

> The marshals came in the early morning darkness, wearing bullet-proof vests and black helmets, heavily armed with automatic weaponry. They handcuffed teachers, fishermen, housewives, politicians, artists, and Catholic priests. For more than a year, demonstrators had lived in tents and little wooden houses on the bombing range.

The bombing of Vieques had sparked the island's *Puertorriquenidad* (Puerto Rican identity) more than any single event since Puerto Rico's rebellion against Spain in the Puerto Rican city of Lares in 1868.

During the protesters' year-long takeover of Vieques, one of the group's leaders, Ruben Berrios, wrote a letter to then U.S. President Bill Clinton:

> Here, next to the idyllic beach from where I write to you, lies a lunar wasteland of unexploded ordinance and depleted uranium-tipped radioactive shells littered about in dead wetlands and lagoons, scorched earth, and devastated marine turtle nests. . . .

In the margins of this letter, President Clinton agreed with Berrios, writing, "This is wrong." President George W. Bush later stated, "My attitude is that the Navy ought to find somewhere else to conduct its exercises." However, even though both presidents agreed with Berrios, representatives from the U.S. armed forces argued that the need for

Navy bombing at Vieques

43

Protesters against the bombing

he clash on the island of Vieques made one thing perfectly clear: For the first time in many years, Puerto Ricans were identifying themselves as something other than Americans. Identity, as psychologists well know, is formed when we confront something that is unlike us. So, in the matter of Vieques, Puerto Ricans told Americans: We are not the same.

—Jorge Ramos

U.S. combat training was more urgent than the immediate and total safety of the 9,300 permanent residents of Vieques. The bombing on Vieques continued.

The protests of Puerto Rico's citizens on Vieques did not mean that Puerto Ricans were not grateful for America's economic help and military protection. The great majority of Puerto Ricans describe themselves as patriotic American citizens, with 3 million of Puerto Rico's 6.5 million people actually living on the U.S. mainland, rather than on the island of Puerto Rico itself. However, the crisis at Vieques caused Puerto Ricans to identify the ways they were also a very unique group of Americans—socially, politically, and economically.

Puerto Rican People

he people of Puerto Rico have not always been a single recognizable group; their single culture was created from a mixture of several very different groups, including the original Taino (Arawak) Indians, the European (Spanish) conquerors, the African slaves, and Americans. Therefore, because Puerto Ricans are a mixture of groups who have previously fought one another, they must find a balance that will allow all the ingredients of their culture to continue to exist together.

Katerine McCaffrey notes that conditions on Vieques have not allowed such a civilized balance to exist. The life McCaffrey describes is one that other American citizens, the ones on the U.S. mainland, have never imagined:

> In Vieques, schoolchildren in starched uniforms laugh and play at recess while automatic weapons fire echoes in the town plaza. People go about their daily routines as helicopters cut across the horizon and warships prowl the coastline. The rhythm of everyday life is punctuated by the thunder of bombs.

Imagine the sympathetic responses that would ripple across the United States if the citizens of New York or California were to protest living under such circumstances. Despite their unbelievable living conditions, the Puerto Rican voices were not quickly heard in the United States because of their Spanish language and their unique culture.

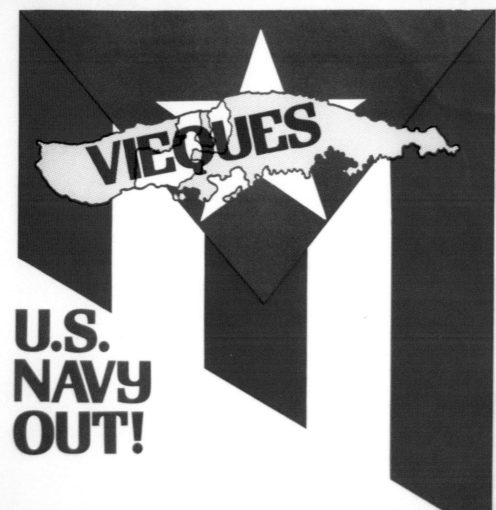

MARCH WASHINGTON,D.C. MAY 17,1980

VIEQUES

U.S. NAVY OUT!

LA MARINA ¡QUE SE VAYA!

MAY 17 AdHoc COMMITTE VIEQUES

Puerto Rican Culture

salsa: Latin American dance music combining elements of jazz and rock with the rhythm of African Cuban melodies.

patron saint: a saint who is believed to be the special guardian of someone or something.

uerto Rico's strengths—its *salsa* music, its brand of Roman Catholicism, and its colorful artwork and stories—are all expressed in Spanish, with some English and African influences. Like Cubans and Mexicans, Puerto Ricans consider themselves *Hispanic* or *Latino*. What makes Puerto Ricans different than Cubans or Mexicans (and other Latinos), is that Puerto Ricans must balance their allegiance to America with their desire to preserve the things they love about their island.

First of all, Puerto Ricans love their *jibaro* ancestors. The jibaro, the farmer of Puerto Rico, reminds Puerto Ricans of the traditions they wish to protect from the influences of the modern world. A typical jibaro is poor, and his home is simple and neat. He is unselfish. Surrounded by an obedient family, he does not complain. He wears his pava, or straw hat, and works with his *machete* (long sword) for long hours in the fields. He is a wise elder in his village. He respects his family and his religion; his home is the center of his social life. As a treasured symbol, the Puerto Rican jibaro farmer has always helped Puerto Ricans take pride in their country as separate from Spain. Now it allows Puerto Ricans to take pride in their country as separate from the United States.

Even though very few Puerto Ricans continue to live on farms today, they remain committed to the concept of *dignidad*, an important value represented by their ancestor jibaro farmers. In today's world, dignidad is expressed by working hard and taking care of all of your relatives and friends.

Puerto Ricans also value their passionate, traditional celebra-

Puerto Rican artist displays a traditional mask.

tions. Each town has a *patron saint*, and there are frequent celebrations on Catholic feast days. During these celebrations, people dance, sing, gamble, and ride amusement park rides. Many carry around santos, small carved wooden statues that represent saints.

Santeria is a set of beliefs that exists within the Catholic religion on the island. The Yoruba people, who centuries ago came as slaves from West Africa, hid their own religious practices and rituals within their worship of Catholic saints. Visitors can see the influence of Santeria during the larger island carnival, in the papier-mâché masks (*caretas*) worn during the celebration. These masks have fangs and suggest creatures that are half demon, half animal. The African influence is also alive in the tales told about demons on the island after dark.

A young Puerto Rican boy plays the drums at a street celebration.

If you were to visit any island celebration, you would be likely to hear a band with *maracas* (hollow gourds filled with beads), which are ancient instruments originating with the Taino Indians. Such a band will most likely also feature a *cuatro triple*, a stringed instrument (like a guitar) from the Spaniards. And finally, the band will have drums of African origin.

The men listening to this band might be wearing *guayabera* jackets, like extended shirts, over their t-shirts. They might also be playing dominoes, placing the pieces down with a quick motion and a loud snap.

Women will surely be walking in brightly colored dresses down narrow winding streets made of cobblestones, past pastel-colored buildings with balconies and tile roofs. The *coqui*, a small frog, is sounding its clear musical notes. Beautiful court-yards lie like bright jewels beyond the heavy wooden doors of all the buildings. Beyond the houses, there are tropical rain forests, sudden short rains, and steep mountainsides.

Almost all the men and women you will see have varying shades of brown skin. Author Robert Santiago notes that, "the slave trade ran though the Caribbean Basin and virtually all Puerto Rican citizens have some African blood in their veins." Also, although full-blooded Taino Indians have now disappeared from Puerto Rico, DNA tests have recently revealed that 60 percent of Puerto Ricans alive today have a Taino ancestor. Spanish ancestry, of the Caucasian race, is the third group making up the mixed heritage of most Puerto Ricans.

Puerto Rican Treasures

ecause of Puerto Rico's colorful blending of different groups of people, skin color is much less important to
these people than to many people living on the U.S. mainland.
No one even considers the marriages between people of different skin colors *interracial* in the same way that Americans on
the mainland consider them so. In fact, many writers have sug-
gested that Puerto Rico's tolerance for all races could be a major
contribution they have made to American society.

These are the treasures Puerto Ricans stood up for when they
defended the citizens of Vieques Island. They wished to save
their past while continuing to make progress as American citizens. Puerto Rico has already benefited greatly from its relationship with the United States, becoming much wealthier than
other Caribbean islands.

Since Operation Bootstrap was established in 1952, 2,600
factories have come to the island. Within the period from 1948
to 1978, the income per person on the island, even adjusted for
inflation, tripled.

However, even though Puerto Rico
far surpassed the standard of living of other
Caribbean nations, it did not achieve the
standard of living enjoyed by most other citizens of the United States. For example, in
1989, the income per person on the island was
less than a third of the average income per person
on the U.S. mainland, and only half of the income
of Mississippi, the poorest state in the United States.

Modern Puerto Rico

uerto Rico has eight senatorial districts, forty representative districts, eleven senators, and eleven representatives "at large," who do not represent any specific part of the island. The Supreme Court of Puerto Rico has seven justices.

In May 2003, the U.S. Army ceased its military maneuvers on Vieques. Most Puerto Ricans felt a rekindled pride in their island. And yet many continued to consider themselves loyal Americans.

Abraham Rodriquez speaks for many Puerto Ricans when he writes, "Of course I'm Puerto Rican. I am also American. I'm both. There isn't a Puerto Rican alive that hasn't been affected by American Culture."

In her poem "Child of the Americas," the poet Aurora Levins Morales shows how she, along with other Puerto Ricans, has had to search through pieces of her country's history to make a single Puerto Rican identity:

I am not african. Africa is in me, but I cannot return.
I am not taina. Taino is in me, but there is no way back.
I am not european. Europe lives in me, but I have no home there.
I am new. . .

Pro-independence march

FREE PUERTO RICO

THE TIME HAS COME TO
MAKE A STAND
MARCH & RALLY TO THE UNITED NATIONS
JULY 25TH NOON @ COLUMBUS CIRCLE

FREE ALL PUERTO RICAN POLITICAL PRISONERS
FREE THE PUERTO RICAN PRISONERS OF WAR
COMITE PUERTO RICO '98 @ 888.509.210

he three political parties on the island are the New Progressive Party (which favors statehood), the Popular Democratic Party (which favors continued commonwealth status of the island), and the Independence Party (which favors Puerto Rico's complete independence from the United States).

Habla Español

dignidad (deeg-nee-dod): dignity

santo (sahn-toe): saint

The Immigration Process

Author Esmerelda Santiago writes:

> I am fifty-eight years old and like a large number
> of Puerto Ricans, have spent half of my life in the
> U.S. and half on the island. My three children live on
> the mainland because that's where they could get a job and
> make a living, and I travel to the states at least once every two
> or three months to visit my sons and daughter. In this I am thor-
> oughly and typically Puerto Rican.

Santiago's description of the continual movement of Puerto Ricans between the U.S. mainland and Puerto Rico has been called Puerto Rico's *revolving door* emigration. In other words, Puerto Ricans come and go between the two places as if they're circling in and out of a building, through a revolving door.

Like Esmerelda Santiago's children, millions of Puerto Ricans have crossed the thousand-mile stretch of ocean to the U.S. mainland. Most of these people hope to achieve the American dream of economic success. But even as these new emigrants arrive, other Puerto Ricans who have already made it to America have begun to dream of the friendly villages and colorful celebrations of the towns in Puerto Rico they have left behind.

In fact, many Puerto Ricans come to the mainland United States with a plan to make money and then return to the island. Santiago goes on to write:

> Even Puerto Rican taxi drivers in Chicago and New York often dream of buying a little finquita in the mountains one day with their savings, where they can grow green plantains for tostones. . . .

Puerto Rican Dreams

oday, an observer at the Luis Munoz Marin International Airport in San Juan can see that the dreams of Puerto Ricans pull them both ways between the U.S. mainland and Puerto Rico. During holidays, the airport fills with emotional family members arriving from all states within the United States. During this scene, relatives are greeting one another in English, Spanish, and a combination of the two (*Spanglish*).

PASSENGER LIST

PUERTO RICO LINE

Puerto Ricans travel regularly between the island and the mainland.

MIGRATION DIVISION • DEPARTMENT of L

BIENVENIDOS

The migration department welcomes Puerto Ricans to New York City.

We can see that Puerto Ricans are pulled emotionally between Puerto Rico and the mainland United States when we notice how much Puerto Ricans have made parts of the two places resemble one another. Since Puerto Ricans have arrived in the United States, they have created communities that feel much like towns on the island of Puerto Rico. In New York City, for example, Italian immigrants have settled in a neighborhood called *Hell's Kitchen*, Africans in *Harlem*, Irish on *the Hill*, and Puerto Ricans and other Hispanics in *El Barrio*.

During the summers, El Barrio has always come alive with the sounds of *La Isla del Encanto*. Also, since Puerto Ricans have also brought their own food with them, the smell of rice and beans, *san chocho*, and *frituras* fill the air. And Puerto Rican flags fly from bal-

In the early part of the twentieth century, most Puerto Ricans settled in the northeastern United States, especially in New York City. Chicago was another favored destination. In recent years though, the Puerto Rican population, along with Mexican and Dominican immigrants, has begun to settle in many more parts of the United States.

project: a group of houses or apartment buildings built with public money for low-income families.

conies, cars, and apartment windows. People meeting one another in the homes and streets of such neighborhoods show a deep attachment to family life, with many young people still seeking the approval of their parents in a traditional way.

El Barrio, also known as *Spanish Harlem*, has become a second home to many Puerto Ricans. Most of its immigrants have always lived in *project* buildings, in extended families of aunts, uncles, and other relatives. They have always spoken Spanish at home and English at school, mourning tragedies together and celebrating life's good times. Manuel Hernandez describes their community as "a warm circle of brothers and sisters who live together in warmth and friendship."

Because they have brought their traditional language, music,

Puerto Rican foods for sale in New York City

uerto Rican food is well seasoned but not fiery hot. For example, sofrito sauce is made of tomatoes, chopped onions, garlic, green bell peppers, sweet chili peppers, and oregano. It is fried in oil, with anato seeds added for color. This sauce is added as a base to rice, beans, or stewed dishes.

The Puerto Rican Day parade

and food with them, many Puerto Ricans who were not actually born on the island, even those who have never even been there, still call Puerto Rico home. Observers in New York City are accustomed to the shouts of "*Qué viva Puerto Rico*" from third- and even fourth-generation Puerto Ricans in the huge annual Puerto Rican Day parade.

Such celebrations have held Puerto Rican families together during their struggles to work and earn money as American citizens. Even though most Puerto Ricans on the U.S. mainland earn more than their relatives in Puerto Rico, they have failed to realize their dreams of economic freedom.

This was especially true during the first thirty years of the 1900s. During this time, only about ten thousand Puerto Ricans migrated to the U.S. mainland, most of them to work in the sugarfields. These workers came to the United States because they were un-employed in Puerto Rico during the seasons when crop harvesting was completed. American companies chose Puerto Rican workers because they were willing to work for very little money. Large American farms actually advertised their desire for "unskilled and inarticulate Puerto Ricans."

Esmerelda Santiago describes Puerto Rico's dream of America during that period as "ghostly as the snapshot crumpled in a migrant's pocket when he boards the jet that will take him to the lettuce fields in California."

Between the 1930s and 1950s, air and boat fares became less expensive, making the thousand miles between Puerto Rico and Florida much easier to travel. Still, Karen Torres-Cox describes the humble way her grandmother, like many other Puerto Ricans of that period, arrived in the United States by boat after World War II:

> The boat was originally used in the war. They used it to bring cattle or some sort of supplies. But when the war finished, they didn't know what to do with these boats, so they ended up using them for Puerto Ricans. And my mother told me she was sick all the way from Puerto Rico to New York. And that as soon as they saw the Statue of Liberty everybody started crying.

Stories like the one of Karen Torres-Cox's grandmother were experienced by hundreds of thousands of Puerto Ricans since the Jones Act of 1917 declared that Puerto Ricans were American citizens.

Puerto Ricans on the Move

Beginning in 1917, the emigration of Puerto Rican citizens to the mainland United States grew at a steady rate and did not peak until the 1950s. In that decade, 470,000 Puerto Ricans immigrated to the U.S. mainland. Not until the 1970s did immigrants begin returning to the island in large numbers. And by that time, many of those who returned to Puerto Rico chose to remain in the capital city of San Juan on their return, because San Juan looks and feels much like cities in the United States.

Many Puerto Ricans go to the mainland to work.

he island of Puerto Rico loses many of its most educated residents because they move to the United States to receive higher pay for their services. This is true for engineers and nurses in particular. Although writers argue about how serious the loss of the island's professionals is, it has become referred to as Puerto Rico's "Brain Drain."

stereotypes: an over-
simplified image or
idea held by one per-
son or group about
another, based on in-
complete information.

Because so many Puerto Ricans travel constantly between the United States mainland and Puerto Rico, they do not have a real sense of belonging to either place. Their problems are unique because the circular movement between the two places differs from that of all other migratory populations in the world. Because of this movement, many Puerto Ricans don't put down roots in either place. Family life, schooling, and income are often severely disrupted as a result.

Also, because Puerto Ricans are the only group of American citizens traveling to the United States from another culture, they face many of the same prejudices that illegal aliens in the United States face. For example, just like illegal immigrants from Mexico, legal migrants from Puerto Rico are often denied jobs, services, and social connections with English-speaking Americans. When those Puerto Ricans who were born and raised in the United States try to return to Puerto Rico, many permanent citizens of the island do not treat them as "real" Puerto Ricans. For this reason, Puerto Ricans traveling from the U.S. mainland to Puerto Rico often avoid the island's politics because they are afraid of being isolated. Two hundred thousand persons who were born on the U.S. mainland are now living in Puerto Rico.

Fighting Prejudice

uerto Ricans on the mainland also struggle against *stereotypes*; these are often expressed by the language people use to describe them. Because Puerto Ricans call themselves Hispanics or Latinos, they group themselves with Mexicans,

Spanish Harlem

A Puerto Rican citizen may encounter prejudice.

Cubans, and immigrants from the Dominican Republic. However, U.S. agencies created these words, and they are not entirely fair or accurate in describing all Puerto Ricans. The term *Hispanic* was created by state agencies after 1970. It refers to the fact that many Puerto Ricans are of Spanish descent. However, it fails to describe those who live on the island whose ancestors were not from Spain. The word Latino refers to people whose ancestors were from Latin America. Like Hispanic, the term Latino does not describe all Puerto Ricans. Many Puerto Ricans' ancestors are from Africa, some from European countries other than Spain, or even from the United States.

The problems of *prejudice* and stereotypes take a long time to solve. For example, there are well-intentioned programs in New York City schools meant to help Puerto Rican children adjust to life in the English-speaking United States. At the present

prejudice: an unfounded hatred, fear, or mistrust of a person or group, especially of a particular race, religion, or nationality.

In addition to the states where immigrants have typically settled—such as California, Texas, Florida, New York, and Illinois—the Hispanic population is also showing remarkable growth in other states. From 1990 to 1998, the Latino population grew 148 percent in Arkansas, 110 percent in North Carolina, 90 percent in Tennessee, 74 percent in Iowa, 72 percent in Alabama, and 68 percent in Utah.

A march for education rights for Puerto Ricans

time, though, many of these programs actually end up isolating the young Puerto Ricans they are meant to help.

Despite continuing prejudice, positive strides have been made, and Puerto Ricans on the mainland and on the island have reason to hope. Puerto Rican Americans have created a rich culture spanning two places and two identities. For example, they have made significant connections with the African American culture in the United States, and they have created their own language, Spanglish, a mixture of Spanish and English. Many Puerto Ricans speak Spanish, English, Black English, and Spanglish on a daily basis. Moving between all these dialects and languages has been called *code switching*. Code switching allows Puerto Ricans to express themselves creatively as they

This Puerto Rican child living in New York will have to learn to switch between two cultures.

are forced to consider all the different ways of thinking that are expressed by the words within different languages.

Tato Laviera's poem "My Graduation Speech" is an example of how code switching—like the physical movement between two cultures—presents both problems and opportunities for growth. This excerpt from the poem suggests Tato's pride in his dual heritage, his struggle for cultural identity, and his fear of the prejudices he faces as he travels from Puerto Rico to the mainland United States, and back again to Puerto Rico:

> *i think in Spanish*
> *i write in English*
> *I want to go back to Puerto Rico*
> *But I wonder if my kink could live*
> *In ponce, mayaguez, and Carolina*
> *Tengo las venas aculturadas*
> *Escribo en spanglish*
> *Abraham in español*
> *Abraham in English*
> *Tato in Spanish*
> *"taro" in English*
>   *Tonto in both languages.*

Habla Español

barrio (bahr-ree-oh): neighborhood

isla (ees-lah): island

encanto (ane-con-toe): enchanted

viva (vee-vah): live (as in, "Long live the King!")

Graffiti in New York's Spanish Harlem proclaims that a "rose still" grows there.

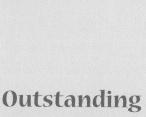

Outstanding Puerto Rican Americans

The Pittsburgh Pirates were playing the Baltimore Orioles in game six of the 1971 World Series. A loud *crack* echoed across the stadium as Baltimore's Frank Robinson hit a ball into deep right field, a sacrifice fly that the crowd was sure would score Merv Rettenmund from third base. But Roberto Clemente, the great Puerto Rican right fielder, known for his "cannon arm," caught Robinson's ball and threw it three hundred feet to home plate, a perfect strike. Rettenmund was forced back to third, and the Pirates held on to win the series. Clemente was named most valuable player of the series, with an incredible .414 batting average, many demonstrations of blazing speed around the bases, and a few remarkable plays against the wall in right field.

Roberto Clemente

MVP balloting: the voting to select the Most Valuable Player of an athletic event.

Like most successful Puerto Ricans, Clemente overcame poverty, language barriers, and prejudice. For example, during the 1960s, he was overlooked for many awards he might have won if he had not been Hispanic. Clemente won the Most Valuable Player crown only once during the 1960s, although he was the dominant hitter of the National League during that entire decade. In 1960, while leading the Pirates to their first World Series championship in thirty-three years, he finished only eighth in *MVP balloting*.

Clemente, who played for the Pittsburgh Pirates during the 1960s and 1970s, had one of the most powerful throwing arms in Major League history. In his eighteen years in the Major Leagues, he also earned a phenomenal batting average, got 3,000 hits, was the most valuable player in the National League in 1966, was four-time batting champ, and, in 1972, he was the first Hispanic inducted into the Baseball Hall of Fame in Cooperstown, New York. He remains one of the greatest players in Major League history.

Roberto Clemente

Rita Moreno

Roberto Clemente rose from his birth into a poor family in Carolina, Puerto Rico, to not only achieve success, but also to stay true to the deeply held values and traditions of his culture. He believed in helping others and giving freely to his friends and family. He performed charity work in Latin America during every one of his off seasons. In 1971, as he was delivering food and other aid to needy people in Nicaragua, his plane crashed into the ocean off the coast of Puerto Rico, ending his life.

Clemente is a celebrated hero on the island of Puerto Rico. The coliseum in San Juan is called Clemente Coliseum. And Major League Baseball awards a Roberto Clemente trophy each year to the Major League player who has performed the most charity work.

Clemente broke down barriers for Puerto Rican athletes who followed his example to make their own achievements. Famous Puerto Rican baseball players include Roberto Alomar, Reggie Jackson (Puerto Rican on his mother's side), and Bernie Williams. Puerto Rican Chi-Chi Rodriguez was elected to the Professional Golf Association Hall of Fame. And great Puerto Rican boxers include Wilfred Benitez and Felix Trinidad.

Rita Moreno

Just as Roberto Clemente prepared the way for Puerto Rican athletes that would follow his success, the actress Rita Moreno opened doors for Hispanic actors and actresses. At first, Hollywood stereotyped her as a fiery Latina, hiding her great talent by failing to give her more complex and challenging roles.

However, Moreno's performance rose above those of her fellow actors when she won the Best Supporting Actress Academy Award for her role as Anita in the movie *West Side Story*. In this film, she played a Puerto Rican gang member's girlfriend, among some rough neighborhoods of New York City. The movie depicted the struggles of poor young Puerto Ricans in New York during the 1960s. *West Side Story* told the story of these young adults, using the structure of William Shakespeare's play *Romeo and Juliet*, with cluttered streets instead of gardens, and fire escapes instead of balconies.

At the age of five, Rita and her mother moved to New York. When she was eleven years old, Rita lent her voice to Spanish-language versions of American films. She had her first Broadway role by the time she was thirteen, which caught the attention of Hollywood talent scouts. For the next ten years, until she gave her powerful performance in the movie *West Side Story*, Moreno played roles that she believed were stereotypical and, therefore, degrading. Not everyone agreed that she should have played in *West Side Story* either. Many Puerto Ricans felt that the play portrayed only the stereotypes of young urban Puerto Ricans—troubled and often violent gang members—instead of demonstrating the complexity of the Puerto Rican experience in New York City.

Freddie Prinze Jr.

Rita Moreno is the first person of any nationality to win an Oscar, an Emmy, a Tony, and a Grammy. While older people might recognize her from her performance in *Singing in the Rain* and *West Side Story*, children might know her from the television shows *The Electric Company* and *Sesame Street*. And adults today might recognize her from the HBO series *Oz*.

Freddie Prinze

he actor/comedian Freddie Prinze transformed his life as an inner-city Puerto Rican into the funny stories he told in his own uniquely Puerto Rican style. By speaking humorously and honestly on such television shows as *Chico and the Man*, Prinze helped mainstream Americans see and accept Puerto Ricans. In that show, the character Prinze

integration: the process of opening something up to everyone, regardless of race, religion, or gender.

played lived simply in a colorful van in his employer's garage where he worked as a mechanic. Yet, because Prinze's character was kind and lived honestly, he broke stereotypes that many Americans held toward Puerto Ricans. Today, his son, Freddie Prinze Jr., stars in many popular films.

Sammy Davis Jr.

One type of struggle experienced by Puerto Rican performers is the prejudice they encounter within their audiences. The singer and performer Sammy Davis Jr. was born in Harlem to a Puerto Rican mother and an African American father. He expressed much joy as he danced, sang, and performed in movies. At the same time, though, Davis, like many African Americans as well as Puerto Ricans, experienced prejudice from those he entertained. Once he became famous, he demanded *integration* in the nightclubs and casinos where he played, both in Miami Beach and in Las Vegas.

Other famous Puerto Rican actors include Rosie Perez, Erik Estrada, Irene Cara from *Fame*, John Leguizano, Jennifer Lopez, Jimmy Smits from *L.A. Law*, and Joaquin Phoenix.

Sammy Davis Jr.

Puerto Ricans in Politics

amous Puerto Ricans in politics, especially those in the U.S. Congress, have not forgotten the struggles they experienced as Puerto Rican Americans. Nydia Velazquez, for example, was born in Yabucoa, Puerto Rico, a small town surrounded by sugarcane fields. Decades later, in 1992, she became the first Puerto Rican woman elected to the U.S. House of Representatives, working for a New York City district that included many Hispanics and other minorities. She won her 1994 election with 90 percent of the vote. She, like Congressman Jose Serrano, also of New York City, spend much of their time doing what they can to help the working classes from which their own families came.

ther important Puerto Rican political figures in the U.S. include Antonio Novello (the Surgeon General under President Clinton), Herman Badillo (the first Puerto Rican to serve in Congress), and Luis Gutierez (who has represented Illinois in Congress since 1999).

Puerto Rican congressional delegation in the Puerto Rican Day parade

Puerto Rican journalists give a voice to ordinary people.

Puerto Rican Journalists and Novelists

The presentation of the journalist Geraldo Rivera is one example of the spicy brand of politics practiced on the island of Puerto Rico. Geraldo began his career as a lawyer, representing the controversial Puerto Rican political group The Young Lords in New York City. He moved on to become a journalist on network news programs. Rivera later hosted his own cable news show and followed American troops to the front lines of combat in both Iraqi wars.

Network news organizations have been slow to hire minority correspondents, including Puerto Ricans. One exception is John Quiñones of ABC News.

Many Puerto Rican writers have helped their fellow Puerto Ricans move to the mainland U.S. and adjust to life there. Rene Marques, the most famous Puerto Rican dramatist, wrote the play *The Oxcart*, which helped people understand the poor conditions in Puerto Rico that led to immigration to the U.S. mainland. Piri Thomas, a famous New York Puerto Rican writer of the 1950s and 1960s, wrote the novel *Down These Mean Streets*, which brought attention to issues like injustice, unemployment, abortion, and poverty. Thomas showed such problems in the voices of real Puerto Ricans, in their own language. Finally, the entire world recognized the uniqueness of the Puerto Rican worldview when Enrique A. Laguerre, a Puerto Rican novelist, was considered for the Nobel Prize for Literature. Another famous Puerto Rican novelist is Pedro Juan, who wrote the novel *Spiks*.

The sugarcane fields of Puerto Rico

nrique Laguerre is the author of a novel, *La Llamarada*, in which the action takes place in the sugarcane fields. His writing is a new type of literature for Puerto Rico, because he explores the places where the poor live and shows the problems confronting Puerto Rican workers. Another similar modern writer is Manuel Mendez Ballester, who wrote *Isla Cerrera*.

Jennifer Lopez

Puerto Rican Recording Artists

Many Puerto Rican recording artists are known for their crossover fame, which means that they were first famous for Latin music before becoming famous for U.S. popular music. For example, Marc Anthony was famous on the island for salsa music before achieving popular fame on the U.S. mainland. An early crossover musician was Jose Feliciano, best known in America for his hits "Feliz Navidad" and "Light My Fire," as well as a controversial performance of the "National Anthem" at a Major League baseball game.

Jennifer Lopez, a Puerto Rican performer from the Bronx, New York, shows the tendency of many Puerto Rican movie stars and singers to honor their Puerto Rican upbringings by expressing traditional Puerto Rican values in their singing and acting. Other fa-

The lives of the poor are described in the writings of Laguerre and Ballester.

mous Puerto Rican singers include Tony Orlando, Howie Dorough (member of the Back Street Boys), Ricky Martin, and the great Tito Puente.

ecause of their strong beliefs in family and hard work, almost all successful Puerto Ricans have given something back to the people of Puerto Rico who continue to struggle. Roberto Clemente gave his life while trying to feed starving people; Rita Moreno broke Hollywood stereotypes that once restricted the performances of Puerto Rican women; various Puerto Rican writers celebrate the beautiful voices of the Puerto Ricans who still struggle in inner cities; and Puerto Rican congressmen and -women work to provide the opportunities of education and advancement.

In "Puerto Rican Obituary," the New York poet Pedro Pietri celebrates both the famous and poor Puerto Ricans of the past who brought their own values with them when they migrated to the mainland:

> *. . . They worked*
> *They were always on time*
> *They were never late. . . .*

Habla Español

Feliz Navidad (fay-leece nah-vee-dahd): Merry Christmas

The Future of Puerto Rico

Puerto Rican musician Rafael Hernandez's 1930s lamento is set to string music and goes:

What will become of Boriquen?
My dear God
What will become of my children
Of my home,
Boriquen, land of paradise?

Puerto Rico's Economy

repealed: officially abolished a law.

petrochemical: a substance, such as gasoline, that comes from petroleum or natural gas.

Kentucky Fried Chicken has found its way to Puerto Rico.

Although Hernandez's fearful prayer about the future of Puerto Rico resembles the sentiments of many Puerto Ricans today, the notion of what Puerto Rico has to lose has changed.

For example, in the 1930s, most Puerto Ricans lived on farms or on large plantations. They could not read, lived in poverty, and had very little say about either the natural or political forces that could destroy them or save them. Today, countless malls and factory outlets extend down highways slowed by traffic jams (*tapones*). Over 90 percent of the island's inhabitants can read. Less than six percent work on farms, but a great number, about 30 percent, are unemployed.

Section 936 of the 1950s economic program Operation Bootstrap, that had once given tax breaks to American companies on the island, has been *repealed*. Because of this, deserted U.S. factories are now decaying around the island. Similarly, the *petrochemical* industry that grew on the island in the 1960s depended entirely on a small regulation favoring Puerto Rico in its oil trade with the United States. Because that advantage disappeared in 1973, miles and miles of empty petrochemical towers line the countryside west of the city Ponce.

Effects of industries leaving the island include an unemployment rate that has risen to 30 percent, as well as secondary problems that go along with unemployment. For example, prostitution, drugs, and carjackings have all become problems for Puerto Rico.

Solidarity with Puerto Rico's Independence.
Madison Square Garden. October 27

for a Bi-Centennial
Without Colonies

madison square garden
Pennsylvania Plaza, 7th Ave., 31st to 33rd Sts.

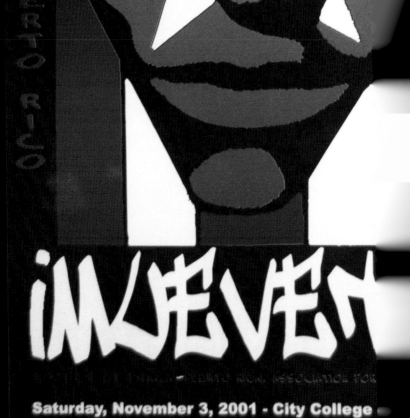

9TH ANNUAL BORICUA YOUTH CONF

NO NACÍ EN PUERTO RICO

INVOLVE

Saturday, November 3, 2001 - City College

Puerto Ricans are building a strong identity.

Because the Puerto Rican farmer and his way of life are long gone, Puerto Ricans cannot return to agriculture to solve their island's problems. Also, Puerto Ricans cannot work in industries that will never return. They must move in new directions in the twenty-first century.

Puerto Rican Identity

he very idea of what constitutes Puerto Rico has changed. Almost 3 million of the island's population of 6.5 million actually live on the mainland United States today, with many constantly traveling between their dual hometowns in Puerto Rico and the United States. Puerto Rico changed during the twentieth century, and Puerto Ricans now have more power to determine the changes that will occur to their society. The U.S. Congress gave the island its last plebiscite vote in 1998, allowing the citizens of Puerto Rico to choose between their island's continued commonwealth status, U.S. statehood, or independence. The choice for commonwealth status narrowly prevailed over statehood, with only six percent of the voters choosing independence for the island.

Puerto Rico's low vote for independence shows that a majority of its citizens believes that their successful future is closely tied to their dealings with the United States, either as a commonwealth or as a state. Puerto Ricans take this question very seriously, with 85 percent of them turning out to vote at the last national election. If Puerto Rico were to become America's fifty-first state, many of its economic problems would be solved. U.S. government programs would then, without a doubt, raise the island's standard of living above its current level. But if Puerto

A Puerto Rican literacy campaign in New York City

"We should not be forced to give up our children's U.S. citizenship so that we can get a fuller measure of self government."

—Anibal Acevedo Vila, U.S. Senate Committee on Energy and National Resources, 1998

An English class

Rico were to become a state, English could become the island's official language, making the island much more Americanized than it is now. Some people think Americanization would mean that parts of Puerto Rico's history and culture could become lost to future Puerto Ricans. Although older residents of the island resist America's cultural influence, such a process might already be happening, as more young Puerto Ricans listen to more and more American music and watch more American television.

The controversy between statehood or commonwealth status deeply divides the people of the island. And any decision made by the Puerto Rican people during the next decade could influence the future of the island forever. Either Puerto Rico remains a commonwealth, keeps its Hispanic culture, and finds new ways to solve its economic problems—or it becomes a state, relies on U.S. programs, becomes more Americanized, builds the many new asphalt roads it needs, and becomes less uniquely Puerto Rican. In either case, something will be sacrificed.

*Education is vital
to this child's future.*

Education

Despite the disagreement among Puerto Ricans on the possibility of the island's statehood, everyone seems to agree that increased education of Puerto Ricans—on the island and on the mainland—is necessary, both to wisely choose the destiny of their country, and to blend in smoothly with American society. However, achieving higher standards of education presents several new challenges. Author Manuel Hernandez writes:

> First, Latino parents must acknowledge the importance of reading and writing. Second, parents must begin by reading to kids at an early age. Third, parents must get involved in their children's education.

"Immigration has strengthened a trait which was endemic to the Puerto Rican personality from the start: our splintered national conscience, our incapacity to define ourselves as a coherent political and social whole."
—Esmeralda Santiago, *Sweet Diamond Dust*

Puerto Rican Day parade

103

Puerto Rican youth, one of the greatest of Puerto Rican "treasures"

One barrier to achieving this is that Latino parents often find themselves working around the clock with little time to attend to their children or their children's schooling. Another barrier is that Latino children often feel ignored in American schools, and they drop out.

Thirty-seven percent of all Latinos drop out of high school compared to only 15 percent of African American and Caucasian children. And education itself is only a first step toward progress. For example, education taught Puerto Ricans to note that they were not only the richest Caribbean island, they were also the poorest group of American citizens.

uerto Ricans want the economic opportunities that all Americans share. But they do not want to lose their traditional love for Puerto Rico, an island that Jose de Diego has called "a jade locket" he wanted to take with him to his grave, an "emerald pinned to the heaving breast of the sea."

Habla Español

lamento (lah-mane-toe): sad song

tapones (tah-poe-nays): traffic jams

Timeline

A.D. 1—Burial grounds for Tibes (pre-Taino) Indians date from this period.

1493—Columbus discovers Puerto Rico on his second voyage to North America.

1508—Spain appoints Juan Ponce de Leon to colonize Puerto Rico. Taino Indians are captured and used as slaves in Spain's search for gold.

1520—First African slaves are brought to the island.

1598—George Clifford of England attacks San Juan. He held the city for a short period before plundering it and leaving.

1625—General Bowdoin Hendrik attacks San Juan with a fleet of seventeen Dutch ships. He holds it under siege for three weeks and then sets the city to flames.

1898—The American general Nelson A. Miles lands troops on the southern coast of Puerto Rico, as the United States attacks Spain in the Spanish-American War.

1898—The United States quickly wins the Spanish-American War, and Puerto Rico is given to the United States by the Treaty of Paris.

1917—The U.S. Congress passes the Jones Act, making Puerto Rico a territory of the United States, and its residents U.S. citizens.

1941—U.S. Congress takes over two-thirds of Vieques island as a U.S. military training ground.

1948—Puerto Rico gains the right to choose its own governor and elects Munoz Marin. He holds office until 1965.

1950—Two members of the Puerto Rican Nationalist Movement attempt to assassinate President Truman.

1954—Puerto Rican Nationalists open fire from the gallery of the U.S. House of Representatives, wounding five Congressmen.

1974—Puerto Rico sues the U.S. Navy for economic damages caused by military testing on the island of Vieques.

1989—Hurricane Hugo reaches Puerto Rico, causing extensive damage.

1998—U.S. House of Representatives decides to allow Puerto Rican voters to choose continued commonwealth status, statehood, or independence. Statehood is rejected.

1999—Two U.S. Marine jets in training drop bombs over the island of Vieques and miss their targets. One person is killed, and four are injured. protesters occupy the U.S. training range.

2000—U.S. federal agents arrest 216 protesters on Vieques.

2001—The Pentagon suspends U.S. Navy bombing on Vieques.

Further Reading

Abodaher, David J. *Puerto Rico: America's 51st State*. New York: F. Watts, 1993.

Aliotta, Jerome J. and Sandra Stotsky. *The Puerto Ricans*. New York: Chelsea House, 1996.

Cofer, Judith Ortiz. *An Island Like You: Stories of the Barrio*. New York: Orchard Books, 1995.

Harlan, Judith. *Puerto Rico: Deciding Its Future*. New York: Twenty-First Century Books, 1996.

Larsen, Ronald J. *The Puerto Ricans in America*. Minneapolis: Learner Publications, 1989.

Ortiz, Raquel and Sharon Simon, producers. 90-minute video documentary *My Puerto Rico*. Ortiz/Simon Productions, 1996. Available through NLCC Educational Media. (213) 953-2928.

Santiago, Esmeralda. *When I Was Puerto Rican*. New York: Vintage Books, 1994.

For More Information

Boricua.com
www.boricua.com/index.htm

Borinquien Online
www.op.net/~ovidio

El Bourica, A Monthly Bilingual Cultural Publication
www.elboricua.com

Puerto Ricans.com
www.puertoricans.com

Puerto Rico WOW!
puertoricowow.com

Sports in Puerto Rico
www.fact-index.com/s/sp/sports_in_Puerto_rico.html

The Heritage and Culture of Puerto Ricans
www.yale.edu/ynhti/curriculum/units/1991/2/91.02.06.x..html

Publisher's note:
The Web sites listed on this page were active at the time of publication. The publisher is not responsible for Web sites that have changed their addresses or discontinued operation since the date of publication. The publisher will review and update the Web site list upon each reprint.

Index

Picture Credits

Centro Library and Archives, Centro de Estudios Puertorriqueños, Hunter College, CUNY, Photographer Unknown: pp. 35, 47, 49, 50, 56, 97, 98

Corbis: p. 19

Charles A. Hack: pp. 64, 65, 69, 70, 73, 75, 92, 102, 103, 104

The Jesús Colón Papers, Centro de Estudios Puertorriqueños, Hunter College, CUNY, Photographer Unknown: pp. 59, 61

Max Colón photo, Centro de Estudios Puertorriqueños, Hunter College, CUNY: p. 55

The National Archives and Records Administration: p. 24

NASA: p. 12

Photos.com: pp. 23, 67, 88

The Records of the Offices of the Government of Puerto Rico in the U.S., Centro de Estudios Puertorriqueños, Hunter College, CUNY, Photographer Unknown: pp. 62, 72, 77, 87, 90, 95, 100, 101

Roxanna Stevens: pp. 15, 17, 21, 27, 39, 53, 96

The Ruth M. Reynolds Papers, Centro de Estudios Puertorriqueños, Hunter College, CUNY, Photographer Unknown: pp. 41, 43, 44

To the best knowledge of the publisher, all other images are in the public domain. If any image has been inadvertently uncredited, please notify Harding House Publishing Service, Vestal, New York 13850, so that rectification can be made for future printings.

Biographies

Jim Stafford grew up on a farm in southern Virginia, went to college in Virginia, and attended graduate school for composition studies in North Carolina. He now lives with his wife, daughter, sister-in-law, and dog in upstate New York, where he teaches writing courses at Elmira College. His hobbies include reading and writing poems, playing tennis, and learning about new cultures.

Dr. José E. Limón is professor of Mexican-American Studies at the University of Texas at Austin, where he has taught for twenty-five years. He has authored over forty articles and three books on Latino cultural studies and history. He lectures widely to academic audiences, civic groups, and K–12 educators.